RAPID GOOGLE ADS SUCCESS

And how to achieve it in

7 Simple Steps

CLAIRE JARRETT

3rd edition, 2024.

CONTENTS

HOW GOOGLE ADS CHANGED MY LIFE

My favourite thing about Google Ads is that it's capable of changing an entrepreneur's life – which is why I have stuck with it for the past 17 years.

That doesn't mean I'm claiming that this book is going to change your life. I'm saying that Google Ads has changed my life, my family's lives, and the lives of thousands of my students. I will prove all of this to you if you choose to delve deeper into my story and teachings.

But I can't promise this book will change your life because I don't know anything about your work ethic or your business – but if those two things are right, then the Google Ads blueprint I lay out in this book will be HUGE for you.

Google Ads is to businesses what steroids are to powerlifters. After managing hundreds of clients and having had many thousands of students go through my online courses, I have repeatedly seen Google Ads immediately kickstart growth and then go on to become the lifeblood of my clients and students' businesses. And I'm not speaking figuratively here – many have gone on to win awards for their businesses after implementing my teachings.

My story with Google Ads started when I was 28. I had just finished a 5-year teaching career and had started a business called Computer Training Solutions – we did in-house Excel, Word and PowerPoint training for businesses.

I was searching for a way to attract customers online because our lead generation strategies were exhausting. I don't think anybody cold calls 100 businesses a day and goes home feeling rejuvenated, do they?

My search eventually led me to Google Ads. I then spent weeks studying Google Ads late at night and then tweaking my website, before eventually pushing "go" on my first campaigns.

They were an immediate hit. My business was filled with enquiries. Back then I presumed I got lucky, but 17 years later I have seen Google Ads work immediately for hundreds of businesses. I now realise that luck is not as important as I thought. Effective implementation is all that matters. A good business idea is not nearly as important as how that idea is executed.

After my computer training company took off, I added Google Ads training onto our list of courses. Back in 2008, I was the first person in Europe to offer them. We did very well, and it quickly became our most popular course. We were constantly fully booked. I trained a small team who would then travel to different parts of the country and train internal marketing teams. Around 10-20 people at a time would go through the blueprint you are about to learn. (My teachings have changed dramatically since. Both Google Ads and my marketing knowledge have evolved in a big way since I first ran my courses many ago. This book will be updated for future Google Ads changes.)

After successfully running my courses across the UK, I became so immersed in Google Ads and marketing that I wanted to specialise in those areas. So I eventually sold my computer training company and started an internet marketing agency instead. We went on to handle Google Ads and SEO for over 75 clients within a few months. This is when I started to really refine the blueprint that's laid out in this book.

This was 11 years ago. I have been managing Google Ads accounts for my business and other people's ever since. I've managed multiple millions of dollars' worth of ad spending and helped my clients to generate billions in revenue, teaching thousands of other people to do the same along the way.

Today, I can easily say that Google Ads has radically changed my life – and everybody around me says the same thing. My husband, parents, brother and 3 kids have stayed in a villa in Spain every year for a month, paid for by Google Ads profits.

Both of my sons now manage Google Ads for other businesses. My eldest is 30 and lives in Thailand. He is the marketing director of a manufacturing company based in China. They have multi-million dollar profits every year – Google Ads is their main source of revenue, thanks to him. He was one of the first people to go through this blueprint 11 years ago, and one of my first agency employees.

My younger son is 21 and is the senior pay per click (PPC) executive for a marketing company. Both of my sons' careers got off to a fast, early start when they were teenagers without college education because they had access to my teachings at a young age. Businesses are lining up to try and hire them both because Google Ads is such an important skill to have.

However, regardless of your age, it's not too late for anybody to go through this book and be capable of dramatically moving the needle for a business. Google Ads has repeatedly proven to be the most important thing for a business's growth. This is because it is without a doubt the most powerful ad platform you can use. (And I've spent over $300K of my own money on other platforms. I've not just "tried" many of them. I've mastered many of them.)

This latest version of this book is the most up to date and advanced version of my teachings. I have continuously refined it over my 17-year marketing career, and you are getting the final version of all that development.

You can sign up for **FREE lifetime updates** of this book plus an optional **FREE Google Ads review** at www.clairejarrett.com/google-ads-book.

CHAPTER 1
TAKE THE REINS OF YOUR GOOGLE ADS

I want to start by telling you why it's so important for you to take the reins of your own Google Ads account, or at least be acutely aware of what's going on.

During the past 17 years, I've come across clients who were letting agencies (and often even Google themselves!) manage their Google Ads campaigns.

I also found certain settings which, when left ticked, increased their average costs by 20% without giving them any more leads. I also discovered automations that wasted their ad budgets on people who would never buy.

More recently, I've seen agencies attempt to use Google's Performance Max tool with small business advertisers, despite the fact it works best with those with large budgets or those in a position to "waste" lots of money while testing.

But if you learn how the platform works, you'll be better positioned to manage the campaigns yourself *or* manage your team more effectively.

This knowledge can mean **the difference between a successful Google Ads campaign and a campaign that drains your cash** – leaving you thinking that Google Ads won't (and cannot) work for you.

In this book, I will show you *exactly* why your Google Ads campaigns have failed in the past, along with the correct way to set them up.

You're going to learn *why* you were unable to compete.

And finally, you are going to become one of those savvy advertisers who you were sure had a secret formula.

MB **Mark bluer**
1 review ⊙ US

★★★★★ 13 Jan 2023

This is not a gratuitous 5 Star review!

I engaged Claire because she literally "wrote the book" on running Google Ad Campaigns. Claire truly exceeded my expectations. What impressed me most is that Claire did not give me cookie cutter advice. She focused on my specific objectives and provided me with excellent advice tailored to my unique ad campaigns. I would strongly recommend Claire to any business or entity that needs to start up or improve its Google campaign.

Date of experience: 12 January 2023

👍 Useful   ⌃ Share   ⚑

> ↝ **Reply from Claire Jarrett**   13 Jan 2023
>
> Thank you Mark, I've really enjoyed working with you on your Google Ads account and seeing the results we've gained together.

RB **Ray Blakney**
1 review ⊙ MX

★★★★★ 23 Dec 2022

Critical to fill in holes in my PPC knowledge

Claire was critical in helping me fill holes, sometimes large holes, in my PPC knowledge.

I am a pretty experienced marketing are know my way around PPC on a high level, but with all the changes that happen and the fact that I have not had a chance to update my knowledge in the last few years I decided to work with an expert. That is how I found Claire.

She was able to figure out what I knew and what I was missing in just the first call and we spent the next 60 days creating successful campaigns which I can now re-create myself. Highly recommended.

Date of experience: 23 December 2022

👍 Useful   ⌃ Share   ⚑

> ↝ **Reply from Claire Jarrett**   13 Jan 2023
>
> Thank you Ray, ,it has been a pleasure helping you!

WATCH OUT FOR GOOGLE RECOMMENDATIONS

A few years ago, one of my eCommerce coaching clients messaged me in a panic.

His cost per conversion had *tripled*. He used to pay £8 for a conversion, but his recent conversions each cost £25.

The market hadn't changed. The customers hadn't changed. His service hadn't changed.

Why was his cost per conversion so high all of a sudden?

I dove in. After a bit of digging, I noticed he had *accidentally* applied a Google recommendation.

That **one accidental click** had modified every single Ad Group.

It added *hundreds* of broad match keywords.

Unfortunately, even though it was easy to apply the recommendation, there was no single "undo" click. Instead, we had to go through the account together and remove all the keywords.

So, I will not teach you how to optimise your campaigns with a single click (which is what Google tells you to do, and their reps will actively encourage you to do).

I want you to be *keenly* aware that Google's suggestions are not in your best interests. In fact, its suggestion to add "relevant keywords" with a single click can be fatal to your campaign!

It will do nothing but waste your budget.

For the beginner, the Google interface can be a scary place. Listening to Google's recommendations seems like a great idea. They appear as if they should bring you more leads or help you to use your budget more effectively.

Even as Google partners, we're incentivised to apply Google's suggestions. The Google Premier Partners, who are the ones Google "believes" are doing an excellent job, don't question the suggestions. They apply all of them. Even when they don't need a bigger budget. Even when expansion makes no sense. There were even rumours that to remain a Premier Partner, you needed a certain percentage of your clients applying these recommendations religiously.

These recommendations rarely work out in your favour.

So in this book, I'm going to show you how to set up a focused, relevant and effective search campaign, step by step. No matter if you own a national business, local business, B2B, B2C, or run an e-commerce website.

To begin with, we'll focus on search ads that will apply for every single business type. If you run an e-commerce store, then Shopping Ads will also be highly relevant for you. In this latest version of the book, I've included a new chapter that explains how to use Shopping Ads effectively. Search campaigns deliver fantastic results to most of my clients because searchers need an answer – and they need it *now!*

We *won't* apply Google recommendations blindly.

Instead, we'll start with one of the most important elements I've seen affect Google Ads success:

Your mindset.

PAID ADS MINDSET

"What do you mean, Claire? What on Earth could my mindset have to do with my Google Ads success?"

In my experience over the past 17 years of managing Google Ads, I've identified that the single biggest factor determining whether your ads will work or not is your mindset. **Your feelings around your ads can make or break your campaigns**.

You can't run an ad for a few hours or a couple of days and then decide that it will not work. **Numbers** are the only proof you need.

> *If you let your feelings get the better of you, you'll make rapid decisions without the numbers to back them up. That will crash your campaign.*

IT IS ALWAYS ABOUT THE NUMBERS

Instead of letting emotions manage your campaigns, you'll use metrics to inform your decisions.

You'll need to identify:

- How many clicks are my ads getting?
- How many visitors are coming to my landing page?
- How many visitors are converting into leads?

If you don't watch these metrics or you look at the wrong numbers, it's very easy to throw your hands in the air and declare the whole thing a failure. *Especially* if you are in a competitive market where it takes a while to get it right.

So before we start this journey, there are **three things I want you to bring:**

1. Courage to see your campaign through.
2. The patience to analyse your numbers.
3. An initial budget to get you through the testing phase.

Yes, Google Ads can bring leads in extremely quickly when your campaign is set up using the method I'm about to teach you.

However, it can take a while for some industries and businesses to get it right. If your industry cost per click (CPC) is extremely high, I won't lie. It's going to be challenging. Your budget won't go as far.

But if you follow the guidance in this book and keep the right mindset, you'll win.

TYPICAL CLICK-THROUGH AND CONVERSION RATES

The two key metrics you will be looking at are: click-through rate and conversion rate.

Before you start evaluating your success, manage your expectations. Your conversion rate will depend on multiple factors, including your industry, location, website, and other factors.

However, these are the average conversion rate ranges *and* the ranges you can reach with professional help[1]:

INDUSTRY	AVERAGE CONVERSION RATE	REALISTIC RANGE
Across industries	7.04%	7-10%
Business to Business	4.94%	5-10%
eCommerce	3.69%	3-5%
Local services	N/A	25-50%

If you're in any doubt about your conversion rate, especially if you're in a competitive industry, please consider booking a discovery call with my team and me. We would love to help!

And remember, don't make decisions based on small amounts of data.

There are many moving pieces within your account.

If you're simultaneously optimising your keywords, landing pages and ad copy, it will take a while to refine your campaign.

But before you test, ensure you're not making one of the common mistakes business owners make in search of profitable Google Ads leads.

HOW TO FAIL AT GOOGLE ADS

In the past 17 years, I've learned how to make Google Ads work for businesses of all shapes and sizes. But I've also learned what *not* to do.

Does any of the following sound familiar?

- You don't learn from your competitors' strategies.
- You don't use your own historical data.
- You make decisions based on small data sets.
- You pause ad groups or campaigns after insufficient testing.

---

[1] https://www.webfx.com/blog/marketing/ppc-benchmarks-to-know/
https://www.wordstream.com/blog/ws/2023/05/15/google-ads-benchmarks

- You change the landing page copy repeatedly.
- You change the ad copy repeatedly.
- You direct all your traffic to your homepage.
- You didn't bother to set up conversion tracking (so you can't track leads).
- You go so deep into the YouTube rabbit hole that you find new Google Ads advice that disagrees with the current advice you're following, so you do precisely the opposite.
- You give up on Google Ads without ever really giving it a go.

All of these are ways I've seen business owners start and get frustrated by Google Ads. Fortunately, I've managed to salvage their accounts, and we discovered better ways to get more leads.

And now that you know what not to do, it's time to see what you **must** do.

HOW TO SUCCEED AT GOOGLE ADS

Succeeding at Google Ads is much simpler than failing.

You only need to do the following:

- Stay positive – a lack of leads can always be fixed through the numbers.
- Read this book thoroughly.
- Research competitors' offers and identify their best ad copy, landing page copy, and keywords.
- If you've been running Google Ads for a while, mine your own account for the data.
- Create great landing pages that give you the best chance to compete.
- Set up your account effectively with great ad copy that matches the keywords you've identified in your account or your competitors' accounts.
- Build a long, negative keywords list to conserve your budget.
- Set up and double-check that your conversion tracking works.
- Monitor your account continuously and optimise it to get even better results.

And now that we've set the scene for your success, it's time. You'll now learn how to apply every single best practice in detail. We'll get into the thick of it with a tutorial created from 17 years of experience, leaving no stone unturned.

I only have one question: are you ready to get started with Google Ads?

I mean – to *really* get started? Leave your prejudice at the door?

Turn what didn't work for you into a lesson?

Yes?

Fantastic!

Hold on to your hat – we're jumping in!

CHAPTER 2
HOW DOES GOOGLE ADS WORK, AND WHY DOES IT MATTER?

Luckily, most people have no idea how Google Ads work – or they wouldn't click on them as often.

You're an advertiser, so you understand the basic mechanics behind them. But if you ask the general public if they click ads, they'll tell you: "No way!"

Then, you look at the way they use the search.

According to research by Varn Media, 58% of people fail to recognise ads.[2]

Google balances a fine line between telling users that results are ads and giving them other options. In some cases on mobile, the ads take up the entire screen.

If you're optimising for organic search traffic or relying on your Google Maps listings, your customers may not even scroll down to see your page.

This is often a problem for my clients with local businesses. Despite doing everything right with SEO, nothing compares to running a paid Google Ads campaign. And through the years I've spent working with them, it has become quite clear that Google has one main priority.

If you can apply it in your campaigns, you can win.

---

[2] https://varn.co.uk/01/31/58-1-of-people-dont-which-links-on-google-are-ads-is-google-making-ads-less-clear/

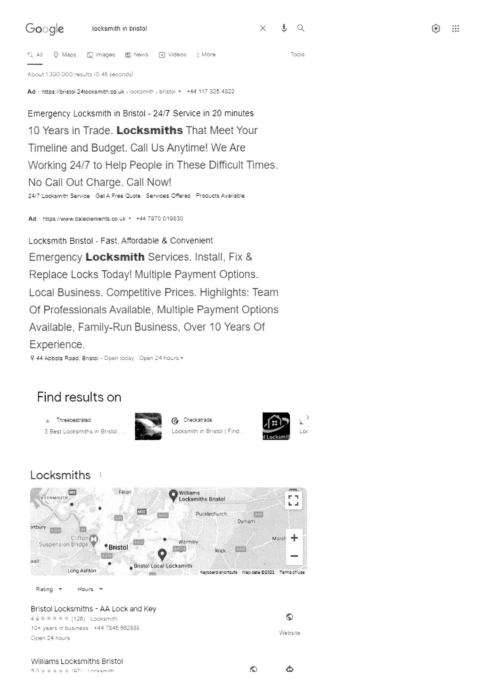

GOOGLE WANTS RELEVANCE

Google doesn't care how long you've been running your business or how great you are at running it. All it cares about are their searchers — how quickly can they find the perfect solution using Google's search engine.

This is fantastic news for advertisers. It allows us to compete effectively within minutes.

However, we need to accept that Google will monitor our metrics and judge us (sometimes harshly). It doesn't want to risk sending people to poor results.

Google will look at your:

- Bounce rate – do people return and repeat the search because they didn't find what they were looking for on your landing page? Or did they exit after the search?
- Click-through rate – what percentage of people who see your ads click on them?
- Landing pages – are your landing pages relevant to the topic? Are they loading fast?

Remember: your ads need to be related to the keyword, enticing enough for searchers to click on them, and your landing pages need to deliver on the promise made in the ad.

In one sentence: your ads need to be relevant.

And now, we're going to start assembling our toolkit to build and launch the most effective Google Ads campaign.

THE IDEAL CAMPAIGN STRUCTURE

Your Google Ads account branches into campaigns. Your campaigns branch out further into ad groups and ads. Most of the magic happens at the campaign level, so we'll focus on optimising your campaign structure in this book.

We'll plan its budget, scheduling and location.

And as I said earlier, we'll focus on search campaigns because they bring in highly qualified leads.

You'll get higher conversion rates than with other campaign types (including Display, Performance Max and YouTube campaigns).

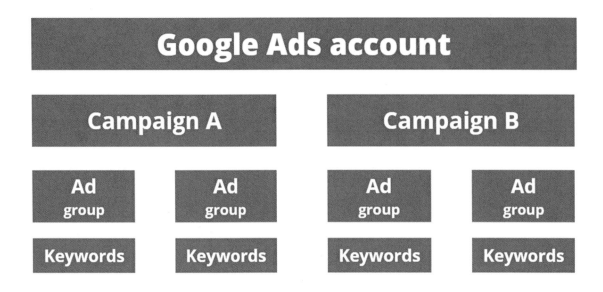

CONTROL YOUR BUDGET AT THE CAMPAIGN LEVEL

> *Claire, I don't want to lose control over my money! How do I calculate the **exact** Google Ads cost?*

Don't worry! Here's how it works:

Each campaign has its own budget.

If you have 5 campaigns with a $10 daily budget, your maximum spend will be around $50 per day.

To get your total daily budget, add up all your daily campaign budgets.

If you have a monthly campaign budget, divide it by the number of active campaign days.

For example, if your monthly budget is $900 and you've scheduled your ads to run every day, divide the total budget by 30 days. Your average daily spend would be $30.

SCHEDULE YOUR ADS

Your Google Ads don't have to be live non-stop. You can schedule them at the campaign level and decide when to run them.

Some of my clients choose to run ads only during their work hours. When a lead calls, the client's staff are there to take the call.

Suppose you wanted to run your ads between 8:00 AM and 6:00 PM, Monday to Friday. This means you'd have 20 active ad days per month.

If your budget is $2,000 per month, divide it by 20 working days.

You'll get $100 – your daily *account* budget to divide between your daily *campaign* budgets.

If you run five campaigns, you'd be able to allocate $20 per day to each campaign.

SET THE RIGHT LOCATIONS

Another thing you'll set up at the campaign level is your locations.

Don't add multiple countries into the same ad. Different countries perform in very different ways; people's behaviours and conversion costs vary significantly.

Ideally, have one country per campaign. You may end up with identical campaigns targeting different countries (and that's fine).

You can advertise right down to the postcode level if you're a local business.

For example, one of my clients is a personal trainer. We were able to choose just one postcode area within London to target with his ads. It was extremely effective – he received two to three leads every day.

While postcode or zip code targeting can be very effective for local businesses, it's typically enough to add the town or city instead.

PLAN YOUR CAMPAIGNS

Great! Now that we've established the foundations, it's time to grab a piece of paper.

Write down a list of the campaigns you think you're going to need based on city or zip code, times of day and other factors.

For example, if I was running a campaign for a business coach who does business in Chicago and London, I'd write down two campaigns at the very least:

Campaign A – Chicago

Campaign B – London.

ANALYSE YOUR COMPETITION

Let me tell you a secret: there's no need to start from scratch with a Google Ads account. In fact, not starting from scratch is our key to success.

(Yes, even if this is your first time running ads.)

It's much smarter to analyse the existing market: who is already advertising on Google Ads that we can model?

But before we move on, a quick note – the presence of competitors is necessary. If you cannot find any when you search in Google or look in other research tools, then think long and hard about using Google Ads to sell your product. Established competitors means there is money to be made in this market. Not finding any is NOT a sign of a great product – it's a sign that your product or service is doomed to fail. Sorry, but that's just how it is.

If we identify an advertiser who's been doing well for a long time, we can see the ad assets they're using:

- Ad copy
- Keywords
- Landing pages
- Locations
- Scheduling.

If we do our research right, we can immediately build a matching campaign. Then, it's time to over-take all of our competitors.

Imagine creating a campaign that **analyses the top-performing competitors** and **takes the best-per-forming elements from each**. You'd create a campaign that's competitive from the very start!

Your leads would come in much faster, even though you're new to the advertising world.

That's what we're aiming for here. And we're going to need a tool or two.

SPYFU

If you enter your main keywords into SpyFu, you'll see which competitors have been bidding for them consistently.

So, for example, if a competitor has been bidding month after month for the last year, you can pre-sume they're making money from that keyword.

SpyFu will also show you their ad copy. If you see the same ad copy come up time after time, presume that this particular copy has been converting well for your competitors.

All you have to do then is take the elements of their copy that stand out the most and plan how to match them.

If you don't have an offer that will compete effectively, there's no point in entering this market.

You may need to refine the elements of your offer.

When I launched my first IT training company back in 2007, I analysed all the existing competitors to see what they were giving away and what their courses included.

I identified benefits and features such as USB sticks, course manuals given to attendees, printed cer-tificates, 30-day and 60-day email support after the course, and other elements.

I took all of these and implemented them immediately on my landing pages.

I was instantly able to become the sum of them all, out-weighing everyone's standalone offers:

> *My competitors had just one or two complimentary products. I offered them **all**.*

- Where can you do the same?
- What parts of your competitors' offers can you use in your own marketing?
- What can you offer that makes you stand out (if you don't want to duplicate your competitors' offers)?

For even more ideas, go back to your clients and find out what made them buy from you.

If you have a sales team, ask them to help out. What do prospects ask for that they've been unable to match?

Don't skip this step. The key to Google Ads isn't the campaigns themselves.

Your *offer* is the key.

And once you find the answers, store them somewhere safe. You're going to need them to write your ad copy and create phenomenal landing pages.

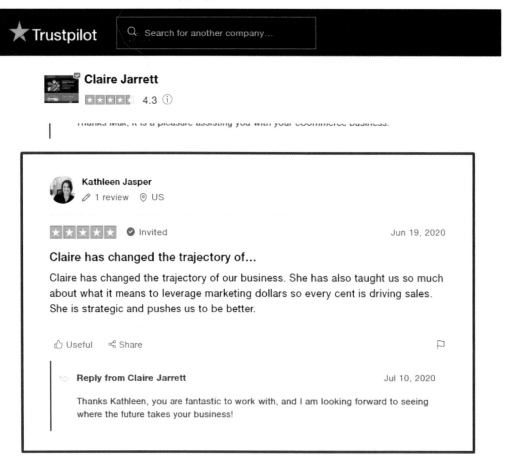

LANDING PAGES

Perhaps you've been using your homepage for all your traffic, and you're not entirely sure why you need standalone Google Ads landing pages.

Unlike your homepage, which explains the details of your business and offer for everyone who comes across it, landing pages are *specific* to your campaign.

They're focused on converting your prospect.

There are no distractions in the form of pages and links (although you can include a select few links so people can check you out a little more).

A good landing page will increase your Quality Score – Google's metric to analyse your ad's quality at the keyword level. As Quality Score affects your cost per click *and* conversion rate, you'll want to get both your landing page and your Quality Score right!

If you're sending all the traffic to your homepage but your competitors have beautiful landing pages, then you need to use landing pages instead. However, if you're in a very small, local market and most of your competitors are using homepages, don't worry for now.

If you realise that you need a landing page, you have quite a few options.

HIRE A DESIGNER

Your first option is to pay a web designer to create a landing page and then clone it.

When one of my clients needed a landing page, I hopped on PeoplePerHour, a freelancer marketplace (you could also use Upwork) and posted a job. We asked for a simple WordPress page template with a few examples based on competitor research.

The client only paid US$150, and the landing page is now converting one in every three visitors into a lead.

Since it was a template, we cloned the page every time we needed it, making only minor adjustments. There's no need to pay multiple times if you request a page that's based on your competitors' best practices.

UNBOUNCE

You can also use Unbounce, which I absolutely love. Again, you can hire an Unbounce page designer to customise your landing page for you for US$150-250 per page.

(A good landing page will convert so much more of your traffic that it'll pay for itself within *days*.)

There's no reason you can't compete effectively with your bigger competitors these days. It's never been easier.

A simple landing page with a Google Ads campaign that follows the guidelines I'm outlining in this book will help you do that.

It will even help you win.

It used to be hard for a small business to compete against big businesses. Their advertising budgets were bigger, and their market coverage vaster. But Google gives everyone a chance to compete. It doesn't penalise you if you spend less or more than your competitors. In fact, I often find that companies who spend more without a clear plan are wasting more of their budget. That's why I love working with small businesses.

Now, I want you to plan your landing pages.

I recommend one landing page per city if you advertise in multiple cities. For a national company, I'd suggest one landing page per every product or service type.

Make a list of all the landing pages you need and then hire a designer.

LANDING PAGE ELEMENTS

Once you've prepared a list of landing pages, look at the elements that make up a good landing page.

HEADING

The crucial element on your landing page is the one your prospects see immediately (and judge you by). We call it the heading.

The heading needs to clearly match your keywords and reflect the term your leads typed into the Google search.

For example, if they searched for "emergency locksmith Bristol", we'd need a heading that says: "Looking for a 24-hour emergency locksmith in Bristol?"

I like to ask the heading as a question because I want the visitor to subconsciously say "yes".

And once their intent is confirmed, we don't want them to bounce back to the Google results. We want to keep them scrolling down our page.

Ideally, they will convert. However, even keeping them on the page for a certain time increases our Quality Score. This is the key to making our ads show and lowering our costs.

BENEFITS AND FEATURES

Secondly, make sure there are some relevant points of text that include the benefits and features of your offer.

You can format them as bullet points.

Don't go too technical. During the first few seconds of your lead's visit, focus on what they can accomplish through these features and benefits.

Break them down to the emotional level. For each benefit and feature, ask yourself: what does it help my visitor achieve?

At the end of each feature or benefit, add a sentence that explains how your reader will gain emotionally from it. Remember that people make decisions based on emotions and then rationalise them logically.

> *People make decisions based on emotions. Appeal to their wishes or fears first. Then provide a logical reason and a tangible benefit.*

For example, a marketing manager looking at a B2B website has wishes and fears. They want to be better at their job and gain respect from their peers. But they can't spend their budget on a tool that promises to achieve their emotional goal. Instead, the tool's landing page needs to tell them about productivity gains and time saved, so they can logically explain their decision.

You can use the PAS – Pain, Agitate, Solve – formula when creating your landing page. First, start with the problem that your lead is feeling. Then, agitate it until they feel it almost physically. Tell them what they stand to lose if they don't solve it.

Finally, deliver a solution in the form of your product or service.

Learn from your competitors. If you've analysed their landing pages, identify landing page elements they have in common and analyse their offers. What can you say on your landing page to convince your lead that you are the best choice?

CONSIDER INCLUDING PRICES

Including prices is worth a separate discussion, and I've had many of them over the years.

In certain industries, especially with services, prices increase conversion rates. Many visitors like to know the price before they commit, so you're more likely to get the lead if you have a price on your landing page. If you can, include prices to increase your number of qualified leads.

However, I completely understand the many coaches, consultants and B2B service providers who prefer not to include their prices. Test your landing page performance with and without prices to see if it affects your conversion rate.

You can also include estimates or starting figures.

ADD CALLS TO ACTION

You'll want multiple calls to action (CTAs) on your page.

Visitors like to convert in different ways, and we'll give them plenty of options.

Firstly, add a phone number. You want leads to be able to call you directly when searching on mobile. You'll also have desktop traffic calling from a different phone.

Secondly, add a form they can fill in to request a call-back.

Consider PDFs or other service materials that leads can download to learn more.

You may want an online chat or chatbot. I use a chat service on my website and it picks up lots of leads for my team. A chatbot can be helpful if your product or service is complex and you have a list of frequently asked questions. In that case, be sure to program your chatbot to provide answers to those questions.

Finally, you may want to include a link to your calendar to book an appointment. This is ideal for coaches, consultants and other industries.

You can track each of these CTAs with Google Analytics. In time, you'll see how keywords affect conversion types.

INCLUDE YOUR KEYWORDS

If you've done SEO, this will sound familiar. Include your main keyword a few times within the landing page text.

Google wants to ensure the page it's sending people to reflects the keyword they've used.

If you don't include the keyword, your Quality Score will decrease, and so will your impression share (the number of times Google shows your ad).

INCLUDE SOCIAL PROOF

Social proof increases conversions, and anything that increases your conversions belongs on your landing pages.

Add third-party reviews like Trustpilot's or other customer testimonials. However, don't link to them. We don't want leads to go away from your landing page.

NO VIDEOS, PLEASE!

Videos are not a good idea on Google Ad landing pages. They can distract people from the other CTAs.

Yes, I've had plenty of clients who have great videos, but in my experience, videos are unnecessary. This isn't YouTube, and Google searchers aren't looking to watch a video. A Google Ads landing page aims to get people to convert as quickly as possible.

Distracting them with a video isn't ideal.

DON'T ASK THEM TO SUBSCRIBE

Don't ask people to join your mailing list or subscribe when trying to convert them into customers.

What's the point of paying per click for visitors who should become customers, only to get them to opt-in to your email list instead? It's certainly not ideal. Your visitor is worth too much to funnel them to a newsletter when they actually want to buy your product or service.

The only exception is inviting them to subscribe as an exit intent pop-up (one which shows only when a visitor is preparing to leave).

YES, IT'S OKAY TO ADD LINKS

You want visitors to have a single-minded focus when landing on your page. However, you can include a few other links in your navigation bar in some cases.

Test this with a tool like Google Optimize to ensure that your links aren't costing you conversions.

And, of course, make sure you track as many activities on your landing page as possible. You can use a tool like Hotjar to see how leads interact with your landing page. And while you've discovered plenty from your competitor research, collect your own data to go one step further with each new campaign.

CHAPTER 3
KEYWORDS ARE THE KEY

Picking the right keywords is the single most important factor in your campaign.

A few months ago, I was analysing an account with an extremely high cost per click. It didn't take me long to realise what the problem was: their keywords weren't reaching leads who wanted to buy.

Instead, they'd used keywords so broad that they reached people who weren't even interested in making a purchase.

As a result, people didn't click their ads.

This led to a very low click-through rate. They received a low-Quality-Score penalty. And as I mentioned earlier, Quality Score is essential.

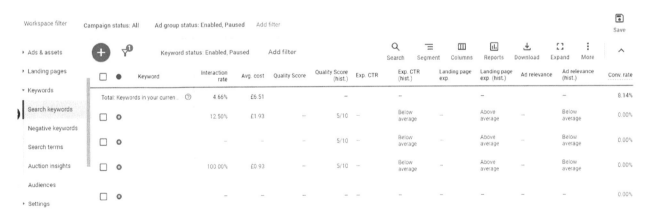

When it comes to Google Ads, keywords are always the key.

But how do you differentiate between keywords and *profitable* keywords?

In the last chapter, I showed you two tools you can use to find keywords your competitors are bidding on. Now, I'll show you how to create your own list of keywords that will help you build a winning Google Ads campaign.

You'll learn how to do it right, and then you'll see the exact mistake this client had made.

STEP ONE - SPYFU

We'll start your basic keyword research using SpyFu (or your preferred tool).

First, enter your main keyword. Run the search. Then, pull out lists of related keywords with more than 20 impressions or searches per month. We'll use SpyFu to identify related keywords that your potential buyers might use, rather than just a handful of highly competitive keywords.

Ideally, you don't want anything with less than 20 searches per month. There's not enough traffic to make the targeting profitable, and, in some cases, these keywords won't even trigger ads. Even the Google platform shows the "low search volume" error message.

Once you've received your list of keywords, export it as a CSV file.

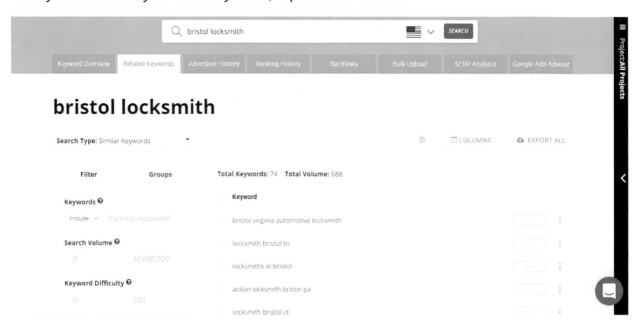

Check each of your main competitors: what keywords are they bidding on? Find out by entering their domain name in SpyFu.

Do this for **each of your products and services**. You might end up with anywhere from 20 to 30 keywords, right up to several thousand, depending on what you sell. If you get many keywords, the next step will take time, but it's essential.

Don't make my earlier client's mistake. Do yourself a favour and don't skip it!

So why was my client using the wrong keywords, and how can you avoid making the same mistake?

When a prospect first starts to consider making a purchase, they go on a journey. In PPC, we call this **the keyword pathway.** The first thing you need to do is **identify which keywords belong at each level of a prospect's search.**

For example, some Google advertisers will bid at the early stages of the decision-making process. For example, if they are selling bikes, they'll target lower-intent keywords such as: "bikes", "mountain bikes", "bikes for sale" and similar terms.

This keyword type appears very early in the keyword pathway and their buyer's journey. The prospect hasn't made up their mind; they don't know what kind of bike they want and how much they want to pay. When targeting these lower-intent keywords, bike sellers will see fewer conversions.

So for the small advertiser, this type of keyword is not worth bidding on. Let's leave them to the giants like Amazon.

You and I need more sales for your business, and we need them *now!*

So what we're going to do is take it one level further. The next step in the keyword pathway is **when a prospect refines their search.**

Now they've identified the type of bike, perhaps even the brand, colour and other features they want. Their search will be more detailed. For example, they might look for "Blue Trek 400 for sale near me".

If a prospect is refining their keywords to this level, we can presume they're getting ready to make a purchase. **It's in your best interest to identify these keywords which signal purchasing intent for your product or service.** When you do, you'll be able to use your Google Ads budget wisely.

Please remember that it's not worth bidding on keywords too early in the keyword pathway if people aren't using them to find a solution.

The lower your Quality Score, the higher your cost per click.

My client's account had wasted *thousands* of dollars each day because Google could see they had the budget to spend, but they chose the wrong keywords.

And even though Google had *told them* their Quality Score was low, they chose to continue running poorly optimised ads.

GET INTO THE MIND OF YOUR PROSPECT

You need to truly get into your prospect's mind and think hard about the keywords that signify potential buyers. Leave the informational keywords (for example, "how to" keywords) to your SEO and blog.

Your Google Ads budget needs to focus only on the high-intent keywords.

Perhaps you now see why I love to work with the business owner when building Google Ads campaigns. You understand your market better than anyone.

I bring the PPC skills. You bring the knowledge of your audience. Together, we can build a powerful lead generation facility for your business.

Together, we will build a profitable ad machine for your business.

SPLIT YOUR KEYWORDS INTO THEMES

One of the worst things you can do if you follow Google's suggestions as a novice advertiser is to place lots of keywords together in one ad group.

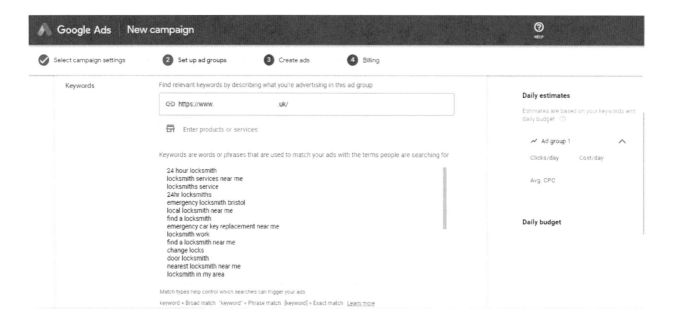

Don't get me wrong – I understand why you would be tempted to do that. The pull to trust Google is strong.

But remember that you will have multiple ad groups inside a campaign. Your goal is to **theme your keywords**. Place similar or related keywords into each ad group.

I've recently worked with a personal trainer who attracted his first three clients during our first week working together.

EXAMPLES OF THEMED KEYWORDS

So let's suppose you were a personal trainer who wanted to attract clients in Clifton, Bristol. You could choose keywords such as:

1. personal trainer near me
2. personal trainer Bristol
3. book personal trainer
4. local personal trainer
5. personal trainer
6. top personal trainers.

There are only a handful of relevant keywords, so putting them all together in a single ad group may work. However, you could also theme them into different ad groups:

THEME	PERSONAL TRAINER	LOCAL PERSONAL TRAINER	BOOK PERSONAL TRAINER (HIGH-INTENT KEYWORD)
AD GROUP KEYWORDS	personal trainer	local personal trainer	book personal trainer
		personal trainer near me	
		personal trainer Bristol	

A different client of mine runs a national business, but he could benefit from local searches too. Say he runs a will-writing company. We'd have sets of keywords for a national campaign:

THEME	WILL-WRITING SERVICE	EXPERT WILL WRITERS	WILL-WRITING LAWYERS (HIGH-INTENT KEYWORD)
AD GROUP KEYWORDS	will-writing service	expert will writers	will-writing lawyers
	services for wills	expert will-writing service	will-writing attorneys
			will-writing solicitors

Each of these themes will form its own ad group.

Did you hear that? This was the most commonly missed section when I audited the accounts of those of you who had bought the 2022 edition of this book.

You are NOT going to put all these keywords into one ad group. You're going to separate each theme into its own ad group.

Then, we could also have locally themed keywords such as:

- will writing near me, will writers near me
- will writing Bristol
- local will writers.

This allows him to reach local and nationwide prospects with highly relevant keywords.

NO NEED FOR SKAGS

You may have come across the SKAG (Single Keyword Ad Group) method if you've done some Google Ads research already. The idea was to create a dedicated ad for each keyword.

However, SKAG is no longer needed with Responsive Search Ads.

With RSA, you can simply theme your keywords. Google rotates the headlines according to the keyword being used by your prospect.

Having said that, there are times when we might add just a single keyword to an ad group if we really want it to shine.

Now, I want you to review the keyword lists you've downloaded from SpyFu.

Add related keywords into a single worksheet and remove duplicates with a tool like DeDupe.ly.

Take out any keywords that do not denote intent (i.e. those that don't show prospect readiness to buy). Remove irrelevant keywords mercilessly, especially if you're a small budget advertiser.

Next, create different tabs within your spreadsheet for different themes.

Group the remaining keywords together according to a theme.

If you only have a handful of keywords, you'll only need a couple of ad groups.

GEOGRAPHICAL KEYWORDS

If your business relies on attracting local customers, this section is for you.

You'll notice two different types of keywords: keywords containing a location and keywords that don't mention a location.

You need to bid on **both**.

For example, a locksmith will bid on location and non-location keywords – e.g., "locksmith Bristol", and "local locksmith".

Your keyword pathway may be less defined if you're a local business. Prospects may perform a search and then immediately convert.

Research shows that people increasingly search for local businesses with "near me" queries[3], so this type of keyword is essential in your campaign.

If you run a national business, you might be thinking this section doesn't apply to you. That's where you'd be *wrong*. Many of my clients succeed by targeting local areas with matching landing pages.

The world may have changed, but customers still like to buy local. Even if they aren't going to meet you face to face.

[3] https://momentfeed.com/blog/50-mobile-local-search-statistics-you-need-to-know-2021/

NEGATIVE KEYWORDS

Most Google Ads tutorials will tell you everything about the keywords you want. In fact, some may make it look like you want every keyword.

That's the wrong approach.

I hope you're starting to notice that there are **keywords you should *not* want**. They'll become your negative keywords – the keywords you don't ever want your ad to appear for.

For example, you may add the following to your negative keywords list:

- free
- cheap
- job
- jobs
- apprenticeship
- apprenticeships
- vacancy
- vacancies.

Adding negative keywords stops your ads from showing for if the searcher uses that particular word in their search phrase. For example, you may want your ad to appear for "personal trainer", but not for "personal trainer job", as that search phrase won't be used by your target audience.

Adding negative keywords will increase your click-through rate. The increased CTR will improve your Quality Score and save your budget.

AVOID THIS COMMON MISTAKE

A widespread mistake I see people make is adding a precise negative keyword phrase that's three or four words long.

There's **no need** to do this.

Just add the negative keyword as a single word.

Note that you ***will*** need to add singular and plural negative keywords. Add misspellings too. Google doesn't see them as the same thing.

At the end of the day, it's just technology (even if Google tries to convince us otherwise and make itself responsible for our advertising decisions).

ADD YOUR NEGATIVES TO A SHARED NEGATIVE KEYWORD LIST

Build one extensive, negative keyword list and apply it to all your campaigns.

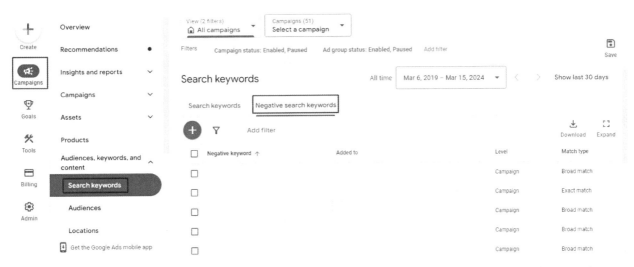

If you already have negative keywords, replace any exact match negatives with single keywords.

KEYWORD MATCH TYPES

Here's the tricky part: keyword match types. Google is very fond of changing match types and adjusting their meaning (HINT: this move increases their profits to the detriment of its advertisers, who would have thought it?).

Right now, there are two different keyword match types you should use: **phrase match and exact match.**

(If you're familiar with the modified broad match type, it's now conflated with adjusted phrase match. The cynical among us wonder why Google chose to do this. Personally, I strongly suspect the real reason behind the ongoing changes is to prevent advertisers from taking control over their keyword matches.)

The third keyword match type is the most common, yet the most poorly performing: **broad keywords.**

A while ago, I had a client advertising a reverse osmosis system. Because they'd allowed Google to match their keywords against broad keywords, their ads were showing up for "Xbox game Rage 2".

(They'd wasted hundreds of pounds because of the broad match.)

Broad keywords will get matched against irrelevant terms, making them a waste of money.

If I were to manage your Google Ads account (and please do take me up on this offer), I'd likely identify many examples of your broad keywords matched against *thousands* of irrelevant keywords.

Unfortunately, broad match keywords lead to a drop in your click-through rate. Your Quality Score then drops and your cost per click rises.

Google's AI continues to peddle broad keywords. Google tells us not to worry; its AI will be able to match *any* keyword against a potential lead or buyer for your service.

> *I've yet to see any evidence that Google's AI can broad match keywords. I only see advertisers wasting their budgets because of false promises.*

It's pushing broad matching so strongly that it's one of the most common recommendations.

"Add broad keywords," it recommends.

"No, thank you," we should say unless we plan to carefully manage the AI.

OKAY, SO WHAT'S THE DIFFERENCE BETWEEN PHRASE MATCH AND EXACT MATCH?

With the **exact match keyword**, Google will only match against that precise term.

For example, if you want to bid on "personal trainer Bristol", Google will only show your ads when someone searches for:

- The keyword phrase "personal trainer Bristol"
- A misspelling (e.g. "personal trainr Bristoll")
- Plurals – "personal trainers Bristol"
- The reverse order of the keyword phrase – "Bristol personal trainer".

With the **phrase match**, Google will look at slightly different keywords. For example, if your original bid is "personal trainer Bristol", Google might match you against "personal gym trainer Bristol" or "fitness coach Bristol".

Yes, sometimes Google gets it wrong. We can end up getting matched against irrelevant terms.

However, this is nowhere near as bad with phrase matches as it is with broad matches. For most of my clients, phrase matches deliver excellent returns.

WHY DON'T WE JUST USE EXACT MATCH KEYWORDS?

> *If exact match means Google only uses highly related keywords, why don't I just use exact match keywords?*

That's a great question!

The answer is that even today after years of searches, 15% of Google's searches are unique[4]. We can't guess the precise phrase a lead will use. People are personalising their searches. They're adding zip codes. They're using terms we'd never have considered.

We're leaving potential search traffic on the table if we only use exact matches. We need a phrase match if we want to allow for these unique matches.

Exact match keywords can also be more expensive, so adding phrase matches is cost-effective.

Of course, we filter out irrelevant traffic by constantly updating our negative keyword list.

And we **never**, *ever* leave our Google Ads accounts unmonitored.

NEVER LEAVE YOUR GOOGLE ACCOUNT UNMONITORED

One of my clients was in a trusting mood. As a financial provider to successful companies, he had a good idea of who he wanted to reach with his Google Ads campaigns, but...

---

[4] https://www.seroundtable.com/15-percent-search-queries-google-new-32936.html

His team had created campaigns with broad match keywords, set their target cost per acquisition, and left the campaign **unmonitored**.

They were waiting for calls from enterprises.

Instead, Google decided to match them against all types of queries. They started receiving more and more calls from small businesses and startups who were *decidedly* not their audience.

All Google had wanted was to optimise for the client's target cost per acquisition. The algorithm sent my client's ads to click-happy leads who liked filling in forms and hopping on calls, even though they were not qualified or didn't have the budget for my client's services.

Perhaps Google had the right intention. But we all know that the road to hell is paved with good intentions. And that's why you should never leave your Google Ads account unmonitored.

Before long, Google will start matching your ads against more and more irrelevant searches over time. It'll change definitions of match types (for example, as I mentioned earlier, phrase match is now identical to modified broad keyword match). It'll introduce updates to its algorithm.

And over time, you'll find yourself with a worse account than when you left it unmonitored. Even if you didn't change a thing except increase your budget.

So keep a close eye on your Google Ads account and regularly update your negative keywords list. In the early stages, this needs to be a daily or at least a twice-weekly task. It's the best way to ensure your budget is going towards the right audience.

And if you suspect your budget is wasted on the wrong keywords, consider getting in touch with my team and I to request more assistance. We'll dive into your Google Ads account and identify inefficiencies so you can make every penny count towards generating more leads.

Her no nonsense approach suits my personality. She didn't ever tell me what to do, but she did ask me some probing questions that got me thinking deeply - and then taking immediate action.

This approach and method is exactly what I needed and I responded very well to this style of coaching.

If you want a coach who nicely nudges you out of your comfort zone so you can grow and explore your potential and capability - I wholeheartedly recommend Claire.

David Nicholls · 2nd
Founder of David Nicholls at David Nicholls Associates
January 5, 2021. David was Claire's client

Claire has helped me create a lead facility that quite simply works. I was having to constantly contact my existing clients and now i have clients come to me which is not only amazing and refreshing but keeps a smile on my face in these uncertain times. I would highly recommend Claire and he skills in google ad words

Kathleen Jasper, Ed.D. · 2nd
Educator | Writer | Entrepreneur
April 30, 2020. Kathleen was Claire's client

In the short time we have worked with Claire, we have seen a dramatic increase in sales. Google ads, Facebook ads, Twitter ads, Linkedin ads make a HUGE difference. Claire knows so much about all of them. She even does our email marketing for us now. Digital marketing is complex and time consuming. I'm so glad we found Claire to manage it all for us.

CHAPTER 4
BUILD YOUR CAMPAIGNS STEP-BY-STEP

Now that you know what to do – and what not to do – I'll take you step-by-step through the process of building a Google Ads campaign that brings in leads from the moment it's launched.

Yes, that **IS** possible – if you've done your research correctly and set up your campaign using the method I'm about to teach you.

First, log into your Google Ads and make sure you're at the campaign level.

(Remember: a campaign is going to be your container object.)

According to the plan we laid out earlier, we're going to set each campaign up with its own location and budget.

Let's imagine we're setting up a campaign for a locksmith based in Bristol.

At this point, we've identified and themed various keywords. We'll set up ad groups for the following themes:

- emergency locksmiths
- 24-hour locksmiths
- commercial locksmiths
- locksmiths near me.

Each of these themes will be one ad group.

Technically, we *could* put all of these keyword themes together, but I don't recommend that. We want a good Quality Score with relevant ads, so we want to create an ad that's 100% focused on each key phrase and its related key phrases.

FIRST STEPS

Click the 'Add campaign' button on your Google Ads screen.

Name your campaign sensibly so that you remember what it contains.

IGNORE ALL ATTEMPTS AT AUTOMATION

We're going to ignore **all** of Google's instructions to add automation.

For example, we'll create the campaign "without a goals guidance" and then deselect the Search Partners and Display Network options (as they'd send our Google Ads to thousands of irrelevant websites).

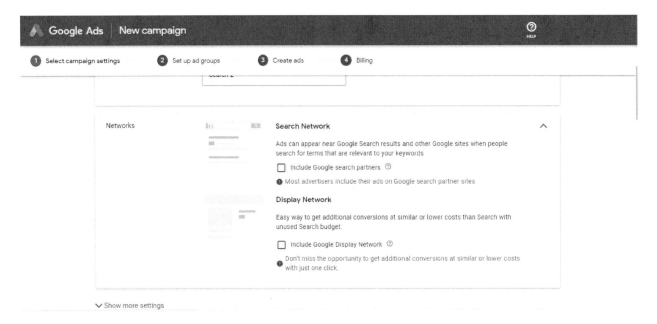

ADD THE RELEVANT LOCATION

We'll carefully add in the appropriate location. You can add zip codes/postcodes, towns or cities, and entire countries.

Some of you may want to add a targeting radius. For example, 30 miles outside your home or office.

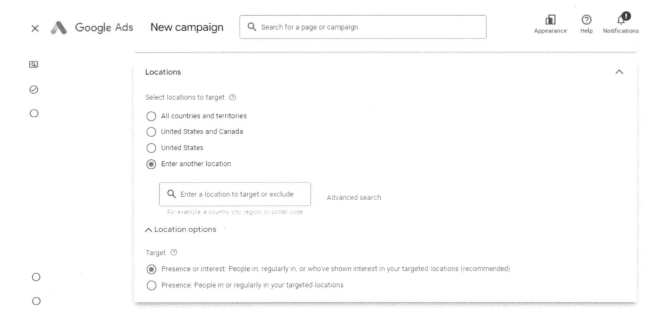

SET YOUR DAILY BUDGET

Set your budget according to your daily requirements. Remember that you'll have multiple campaigns, so you need to divide the budget between your campaigns.

If you have three campaigns and a $300/day budget, consider allocating $100 per day to each campaign.

In this latest version of the book, we are going to put Google in charge of the bidding by selecting Maximise Conversions.

Most advertisers will now use Maximise Conversions and/or Target CPA (an automatic bidding strategy based on a target cost per action that you set) even in the early stages, as Google has data from other advertisers. The cost per conversion will improve over time, as it gathers historical ad performance data, and as you add more negative keywords. As you run ad campaigns, the AI will start to "learn" how your ads perform, and your ad costs will drop.

My team and I often use Maximise Conversions to begin with, and then add a Target CPA as we begin to understand the cost we are paying for a conversion.

SCHEDULE YOUR ADS

You'll find the option to schedule your ads hidden in the "More settings" option.

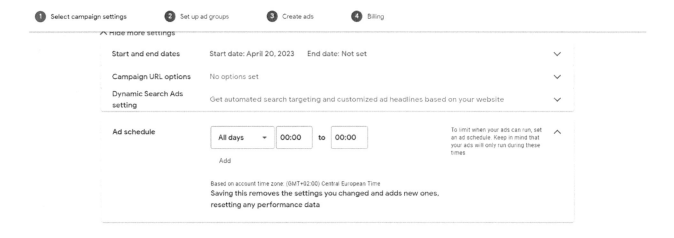

If you're a B2B advertiser, you may want to choose 8:00 AM to 6:00 PM, Monday to Friday.

If you don't have anyone to answer your phone out of hours, you can turn your ads off. You will likely find that many of your competitors turn their ads off during evenings and weekends.

However, if you can provide service during that time, it can be an excellent opportunity for small advertisers.

WHAT SHOULD YOU BID?

As you've selected Maximise Conversions, you won't be asked to enter a bid. Instead Google will bid to try and bring in as many leads as possible for you within your budget.

CREATE YOUR FIRST AD GROUP

After setting up the basics, you'll be taken into creating your first ad group.

Name it according to your keyword theme. In our example, we'll use "Emergency Locksmith".

Go back to your spreadsheet and identify your keywords that fit this theme.

In our example, we would have:

- emergency locksmith
- emergency locksmith near me

· emergency locksmith Bristol.

We'll also add other related keywords containing the word "emergency" that we found earlier in our research.

It's optional to add singular and plural keywords. Google will match them anyway, so you technically don't need them. However, I occasionally see slight differences in Quality Score with singular vs plural.

ADD EXACT AND PHRASE KEYWORDS ONLY

Add both the exact and phrase versions of your chosen keywords, but make sure you don't add your broad keywords unformatted.

You can control the match type with formatting:

- keyword = Broad match
- "keyword" = Phrase match
- [keyword] = Exact match.

It should look like this:

- "emergency locksmith"
- "emergency locksmith near me"
- "emergency locksmith Bristol"
- [emergency locksmith]
- [emergency locksmith near me]
- [emergency locksmith Bristol].

CREATE YOUR AD

Expanded text ads are no longer supported. You can only create Responsive Search Ads (RSAs).

When RSAs first launched, I didn't really like them. However, I've grown to love them. For a geek like me, it's very satisfying to optimise them until you get an excellent score.

To create your RSAs, we'll need to enter a variety of headlines and descriptions to achieve a good or excellent score.

< >

Add a final URL to see headline and
description suggestions

Ad strength ⑦
Incomplete

○ Add headlines   View ideas
○ Include popular keywords   View ideas
○ Make headlines unique   View ideas
○ Make descriptions unique   View ideas

Assets can be shown in any order, so make sure that they make sense individually or in
combination, and don't violate our policies or local law. Some shortening may also occur in some
formats. You can make sure certain text appears in your ad. Learn more

⚠ Because you selected **phone calls** as
a campaign goal, add a call asset to
use with your ads.

+ Calls

T⊤ Headlines 0/15 ⑦   View ideas   ︿

Headline	
Required	0 / 30

Headline	
Required	0 / 30

Headline	
Required	0 / 30

Add as many headlines and descriptions as possible to achieve an excellent score.

Google specifically wants you to **use keywords** in your ad, plus other unique items that it can use to
build a winning ad. You'll need to have a variation of each keyword you're bidding on in your ad headline and descriptions.

However, **Google doesn't want you to repeat yourself.** Add in elements of your unique selling prop-
osition, benefits and features. Reference the competitor research you did earlier:

- What element of your competitors' offers stands out in their ads?
- Where can you make your offer better than their offers?

Once you achieve an excellent score, you'll be able to get a great Quality Score.

SHOULD YOU PIN HEADLINES?

I don't recommend pinning headlines unless you *absolutely* need to.

When you pin headlines, you force Google to show one of your headlines in a certain position. Google
hates it when you do this; it wants to freely rotate all the headlines and descriptions to find winning
combinations.

You'll see your ad preview on the right-hand side as you build your ads. Keep an eye on it and ensure the combinations make sense.

AD COPY TIPS

Use numbers wherever possible in your headlines – e.g. discounts as a percentage or the amount off the normal price. Consider using other impacting numbers as well, like your number of 5-star testimonials.

Feel free to do the same in your descriptions.

ADD TESTIMONIALS

The best ad copy tip I can share is to include testimonial snippets. They'll appear under the main elements of your ad.

Use this space to insert brief testimonials, such as "Company X did an amazing job. I would highly recommend them!"

Then, add the client's name.

Make sure that the testimonial you use can be found and verified on your landing page. In fact, make sure every claim you make in your ad copy is confirmed somewhere on your landing page. Otherwise, you may frustrate visitors and encourage them to hit the back button.

Once you get a good or excellent score on your ad, move on.

At this stage, Google will tell you how many clicks per day it thinks you could get.

Pay attention to this, especially if it's telling you zero because it thinks you can't get any traffic. Sometimes, this happens because you've chosen highly focused keywords. I've had this happen in local campaigns, but they have still had great results.

If your keywords are grounded in research, hit "Publish" anyway.

AD EXTENSIONS

Google may ask you to create ad extensions before you publish your campaign. I prefer to add them later manually, as I have more control.

Ad extensions are additional elements that appear within your ads. For example, links to other pages on your website, call extensions, etc. Google likes them, and it'll typically show the extensions that get the highest click-through rates.

It's worth testing and adding a variety of ad extensions, such as:

- Sitelinks
- Call extensions
- Structured snippets
- Price extensions
- Promotion extensions
- Image extensions.

In fact, they're *so* valuable that I'll walk you through each one!

SITELINKS

Sitelinks are links within your site that take your visitor to a different landing page. Please remember this essential piece of information because...

I often see advertisers whose sitelinks take people to information-scarce pages that barely offer them the option to convert. If your landing page is set up to convert visitors and you've added sitelinks that take people to random pages on your site, you could lose leads!

Carefully consider what you want people to do and optimise your sitelink pages as landing pages.

Don't follow the crowd and copy blindly. Only add relevant sitelinks. Otherwise, they can be one of the biggest drains on an advertiser's budget, leading to colossal conversion losses. If you add sitelinks, seriously consider offering a CTA on those pages.

For example, send visitors to book a consultation or a visit.

STRUCTURED SNIPPETS

The next extension type I recommend is structured snippets, which you'll find under "Assets" in the left-hand menu. Select "Structured snippets" and you'll be able to add snippets to existing campaigns. Most advertisers add service or location snippets.

Use your structured snippets as a place to reinforce the different services that you offer.

They won't significantly increase your CTR, but even a small percentage increase makes them worth adding.

CALL EXTENSIONS

Most businesses add call extensions. If you're a local business, include a local number.

Many of my clients purchase additional numbers for each Google Ads campaign. They all re-divert to the main switchboard.

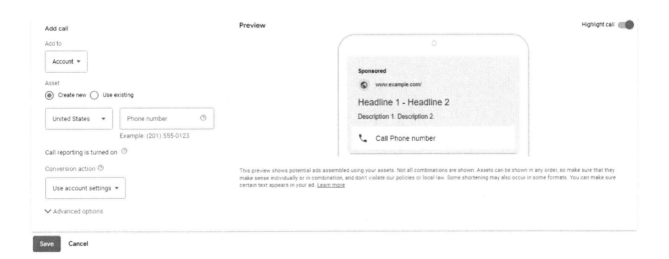

This works particularly well in local campaigns that are using local landing pages. I've seen 800 or 0800 numbers work well too.

LOCATION EXTENSIONS

Location extensions work well for local businesses, especially if you want to attract physical visits or prove that you're genuinely local or have an office in the area.

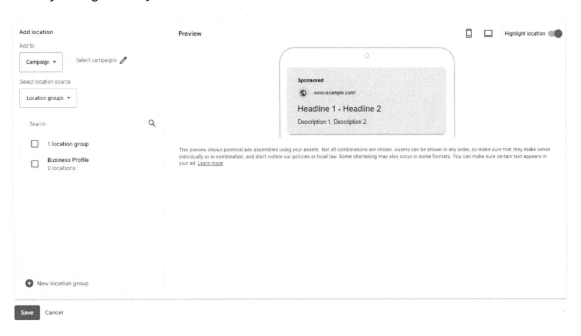

PRICE EXTENSIONS

If you're willing to display prices publicly or you're very competitive, use price extensions.

PROMOTION EXTENSIONS

Promotion extensions are ideal for time-specific offers, such as Black Friday, where you can give an offer code to your leads. Include a start date and end date and use a specific offer code to track your leads and sales.

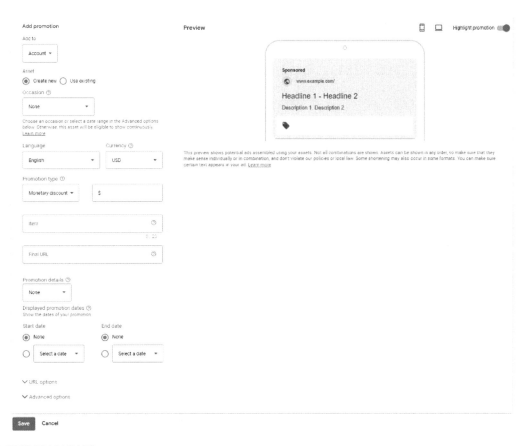

IMAGE EXTENSIONS

Image extensions look great and vastly increase CTR.

They're ideal for local businesses, coaches, consultants and other services where you can upload a photo of your team delivering your service.

DEVICE BIDS

This section is less relevant in this 2024 edition, as using Target CPA bidding means device bids will be removed by Google. If you are deciding to control your bidding manually, then this section still applies.

You could refine the devices section to specify the devices where your ads will be shown (especially if you are in a B2B industry).

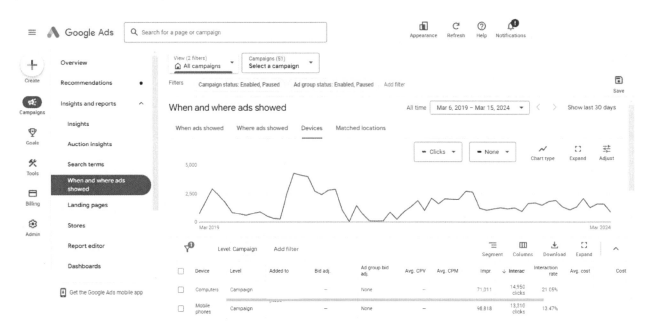

For example, some of my clients have had great results from changing bids to target desktop traffic. You can do this by adjusting the mobile bid to -100%.

If you're in an emergency business or you're a local business, most of your clicks and conversions will come directly from mobile traffic, so you could increase the bidding on mobile.

With your campaign built, you're 99% ready to get started with your Google Ads success!

But once your leads start pouring in, we need to talk about one very important aspect of running a successful Google Ads campaign: **tracking**.

CHAPTER 5
TRACKING YOUR CAMPAIGNS

Like you, I can't wait to see you start bringing in those leads and sales. I'm proud of every client who experiences the incredible benefits of Google Ads.

In some cases (like in the example you're about to see), my clients had to ask me to pause their campaign. They were so successful that they got more leads than they could handle!

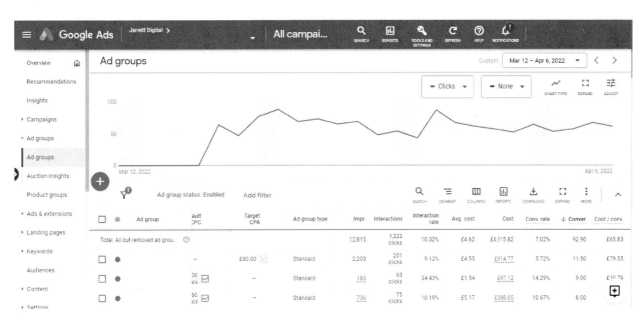

In this client's case, direct telephone leads weren't being tracked, so their cost per conversion looked higher than it actually was. And that leads me to one very important point...

Before Google sends leads your way, we need to ensure you can track your results. This is especially important as it is using the conversion data to control your bidding. If Google cannot see the leads, it won't know which keywords are working for you.

WHAT SHOULD YOU TRACK?

We'll track all the ways your prospects can convert. For example, we might track:

1. Mobile phone calls
2. Form completions (especially a call request)
3. Appointment bookings
4. Online chats
5. Purchases (including the amount)
6. PDF downloads (or a gated lead magnet that requires your prospects to provide you with their contact details)
7. Booking a demo
8. Booking a free trial
9. Scroll depth (how far your prospects scroll down your landing page).

In most cases, you don't need to track scroll depth. But it can be helpful if you have a long sales cycle.

This list is by no means exhaustive If you need help with tracking, my team and I offer this service. 99% of our clients have issues with conversion tracking – it's very common to need expert help to get this sorted. Get in touch if you want to discuss this at our website at www.clairejarrett.com/contact.

Remember – tracking helps you to continuously optimise your Google Ads account and is how Google will control your bids. If you thought a 20% conversion rate at a few pounds per conversion was good, just imagine what you could achieve by fine-tuning every aspect of your Google Ads account!

HOW TO START TRACKING CONVERSIONS

There are plenty of ways to track conversions. You could do it via Google Analytics and then import them to Google Ads. You could track them directly via Google Ads.

You can also use tracking software like Hyros, Wicked Reports, HubSpot and others for more complex situations. They add extra layers of data, such as sales amounts and sales cycle stages to give you complete visibility.

Right now, I want you to make sure you have an up-to-date version of Google Analytics on your website, preferably installed via Google's Tag Manager.

This may sound complicated, but you can get a specialist to do this for you at an affordable price.

Personally, I prefer HubSpot. Even the basic versions of it will tie in web tracking with each marketing element, so you can track which of your ads referred specific contacts.

You can also assign deals or sale amounts to each contact as you close them to get a crystal-clear picture of your marketing ROI.

HOW TO CHECK IF YOUR TRACKING WORKS

This book aims to help you to get your campaign launched, track leads and make money – but that's only the beginning. Once your campaign starts generating revenue, you'll be ready to scale it!

We need to make sure that you're ready for scaling by accurately tracking your conversions.

I like to use the Tag Assistant Legacy plugin to check if the tracking tags are working **before** launching a Google Ads campaign.

Simply add the Chrome plugin, test your forms (or other conversion actions), and check if the conversion tracked.

Don't skip this step! Without clear insights into your conversions, you can't optimise your ad campaigns. And if you can't see what's triggering your conversions, you can't make your campaign even better.

SET YOUR ADS LIVE

Drumroll please... It's time to set your ads live! But before you bring out the confetti, we need to enable your campaigns in your Google Ads account.

Click "enable" on each campaign in your account, one by one.

If you've paused ads or keyword groups inside your campaigns or ad groups, they will stay paused. Setting your campaign live won't unpause other objects within it.

SPY ON YOUR TRAFFIC IN REAL TIME

Once your ads are live, you'll need to keep a close eye on your account daily. A brand-new account or new campaigns need very careful monitoring.

Since I want to spot any problems as they arise, I use a tool that allows me to 'spy' on my campaign traffic in real-time. I can check how many (and which) pages my visitors use and I spot problems quickly. Even if there are errors (such as sending visitors to the wrong page or 404 "Page not found" errors), I can see and fix them before they affect my results.

My favourite tool for spying on traffic is Improvely – which you can find at www.improvely.com. Improvely and HubSpot can track when visitors sign up, the pages they visit and the emails they read. You can also use the live form of Google Analytics.

(Of course, not everyone is a geek like me who enjoys seeing clicks and conversions pouring in in real-time).

I've found that saying "I can see you're interested in product X, how can I help?" really impresses prospects. You'll already know what your prospect wants when they hop on a call.

You may want to take this one step further and reach out proactively to prospects who signed up for a lead magnet but who haven't booked a call. I like to send them an email or even hop on a call if I have their number.

START THINKING ABOUT YOUR QUALITY SCORE

Once your ads have been live for a couple of days, you should be able to see your Quality Score (depending on your number of ad impressions).

If you've been running your account for a while using the same or similar keywords, this can affect your keyword Quality Score in your new campaigns. It *will* update, but it'll take a while. Google promises that this happens in real-time, but I haven't experienced it.

Google definitely 'punishes' people who've been doing a bad job with their Google Ad accounts. Even if it's because of following Google's own recommendations. Go figure!

ADD YOUR QUALITY SCORE COLUMNS

You can add your Quality Score columns in the Audiences, keywords, and content tab, under "Columns". Add your Expected CTR, Landing page experience and Ad relevance.

These 3 metrics will form the basis for Google's assessment of your Quality Score.

QUALITY SCORE ELEMENT #1 – CLICK-THROUGH RATE

The most important element of your Quality Score is the click-through rate.

You can even overcome a poorly optimised landing page if you get a great CTR by creating great ads with stand-out offers (although you'd still suffer from a low conversion rate on the page, of course!)

QUALITY SCORE ELEMENT #2 - AD QUALITY

Google assesses how well you set up your Responsive Search Ads and if they're a match for your key-words. Based on its assessment, it shows you your Ad Quality score.

Your score should always be great, based on what I've taught you so far. If not, it's time to go back and revisit Chapter 4, pronto!

QUALITY SCORE ELEMENT #3 - LANDING PAGE

Your landing page affects your Quality Score the least.

Still, you want to make sure it's optimised – if not to increase your Quality Score, then to convert more prospects.

First, **make sure your landing page is relevant to your keywords.** If you offer different services and products, create dedicated landing pages that meet the intent of each keyword. A neat trick I like to use is to create a dedicated landing page for each keyword theme/ad group.

Have a keyword in your landing page headline and keywords in your website copy. It reinforces the searcher's intent and confirms that, yes, they've come to the right place!

Finally, don't forget about **the technical details**. Your landing page needs to load fast, which you can check with Google's PageSpeed Insights tool. And if your campaigns reach mobile searchers, make sure they load correctly on their phones.

Google wants to see **a low bounce rate**. This means that visitors don't exit your landing page and go back to the search results. Instead, Google wants them to stay on your page and uses that to gauge quality.

It also checks whether your landing page reflects your target keywords.

If you want to bid on competitors' names and products, you could end up with a low Quality Score because your site isn't actually... you know... your competitors' site!

One way to circumvent that is to build a product or service comparison page – i.e. your product vs their product, perhaps with a table that shows why yours is better.

HOW TO SAFELY CHECK YOUR ADS

I know you're excited to see your ads. But the number one thing you should NOT do is hunt for them.

Why?

Because you'll increase your impressions, drop your CTR and lower your Quality Score.

This is because, of course, you will try *not* to click on your ads because every click costs you money. And not clicking is the opposite of what you want your prospects to do.

Make sure you ask your team not to click your ads as well. I've had many business owners tell me that their team has been clicking their own ads without realising it.

The best way to check that your ads are showing is to look at the "Status" column in your Google Ads account. You can also use Google's Ad Preview tool to see which spots they appear in. There's no need to do it manually (and ruin your Quality Score).

If your ads aren't showing, the Ad Preview tool displays a list of keywords it could have been matched against, along with the reasons they didn't show.

You'll discover issues such as:

- Ad scheduling
- Negative keywords
- Wrong keyword match type
- Budget (Google divides your budget up through the day, so if it thinks you'll run out, it won't show your ads all the time).
- Billing details (your card may have stopped working, and you need to add a backup).
- Quality Score (Google thinks your ad isn't good enough to appear in the top results).
- Bid (Google thinks your bid isn't high enough to get into the top results).
- Trademark issues (you won't be able to include a trademarked term in your ads, even if it's your own – contact the government department that you registered your trademark with and let them know your Google Ads Account ID so they allow your account to use it).
- Other issues (there may be issues linked to your market, depending on what you sell).

Test your ads in a few different areas when using the Ad Preview tool – even right down to the post-code. Avoid searching at the country level; most searches won't show up.

LAUNCH DAY CHECKLIST – WHAT SHOULD I CHECK?

On the day you launch your Google Ads, you'll want to double-check your campaigns. It's incredible how many things can go wrong, like web designers accidentally overwriting codes and other simple mistakes.

Here's how to have a mistake-proof launch day:

1. Check your billing details and consider adding a backup credit card.
2. Check several of your keywords in the Ad Preview Tool, following the previous instructions.
3. Test your landing page load times on desktop and mobile.
4. Check your landing pages – do the buttons work? Can your leads fill in the forms?
5. Check your conversion tracking codes.
6. Check the live version of Google Analytics.

If you get a lot of traffic, you may even want to keep your Google Analytics open throughout the day.

Ultimately, your launch day checklist should make sure there aren't any overlooked mistakes. The majority of your campaign set-up work should have happened earlier.

If you're not confident about getting this all set up correctly, and would prefer an expert to manage it for you or help you with this, I'm here to help. Book a call with me at www.clairejarrett.com/contact. My team and I would love to assist you in setting up effective Google Ads campaigns – without the headaches.

CHAPTER 6
MONITORING AND OPTIMIZING YOUR ACCOUNT

During the first few days of your campaign, check your account daily. Over time, you can change the frequency to weekly, but the first few days are *essential*.

Check your search terms. Add negative keywords. Do these things at the account level or check each campaign and ad group. Reduce any negative keywords to single broad keywords. Add them to your shared negative keyword list and check that they apply at the Account level.

It's very easy to accidentally add negative keywords to individual ads or campaigns and to get confused because your other ads are still targeting those negative keywords.

Re-check your launch day checklist items from Chapter 6 to ensure your landing pages and conversion tracking work properly.

TROUBLESHOOTING GUIDE: "HELP, I'M NOT GETTING ANY CONVERSIONS!"

If you're not getting leads, remember that the issue could be caused by different factors. Ask yourself the following questions to troubleshoot:

1. Are you spending enough for a thorough test?
2. Does your landing page convert visitors effectively?
3. Are the keywords you're paying for relevant?
4. Is your conversion tracking working correctly?

ARE YOU SPENDING ENOUGH?

Is your daily budget big enough to bring in enough clicks?

A reasonable conversion rate will be 5% to 10% if you advertise a local business. This means you will need 10 to 20 clicks to get a lead.

If your competitors bid $5 on average and you only bid $2, then you won't get enough clicks in the top spots.

Consider raising your bids and your daily budget.

IS YOUR LANDING PAGE CONVERTING?

You'll need to refine your landing page and consider creating additional landing pages for specific keywords.

If you're getting clicks, but your landing page isn't converting, consider having your landing page audited by a professional.

There are services available that will perform this for you—I have personally used www.conversionwise.com/audits/ and recommend them to clients.

ARE YOUR KEYWORDS RELEVANT?

If you've added lots of exact and phrase-match keywords, you could be matched against irrelevant traffic. Check your search terms.

Also, carefully consider your keywords and if they're genuinely relevant. Is it possible they're not keywords used by people who are ready to buy from you?

If your keywords don't represent your buyer's intent, consider pausing them.

IS YOUR CONVERSION TRACKING WORKING?

Double-check your conversion tracking if you're getting leads but they don't seem to originate from Google Ads.

Is it possible you're getting leads, but they're not showing up in your metrics? Double and triple check your tracking set-up to be sure.

OPTIMISATION CHECKS: "I'M GETTING CONVERSIONS! NOW WHAT?"

Great news, you're getting conversions!

Next up: how do you get more of them at a lower cost?

There are five things you can consider at this stage.

1. Peel and stick keywords
2. Quality Score
3. Impression share and click share
4. Adding tons more negative keywords
5. Editing the bidding.

Let's look at each in turn.

1. PEEL AND STICK KEYWORDS

When analysing search terms, you'll find keyword phrases worth targeting separately.

If you isolate them into a separate ad group and create a matching ad, you'll get more conversions. Plus, you'll see an increase in your Quality Score.

We call this method "peel and stick". If you spot one (or more) of these terms, create a new ad group in the same campaign and a targeted Responsive Search Ad.

Yes, you can add the keyword to an existing ad group, but you'll see far better results with a new ad group.

2. QUALITY SCORE

Improving your Quality Score is an ongoing task. It may rapidly update, especially if you've been advertising for some time. I've seen many advertisers suddenly penalised with a low Quality Score, with their keywords barely triggering their ads.

What can cause a low Quality Score?

There are many reasons, but I primarily look for the following when auditing an account:

ARE YOU BIDDING ON COMPETITOR NAMES?

This can be very difficult to get right. You may have to accept that you will never get a good Quality Score because at the end of the day, your visitor wants your competitor's website, not yours.

ARE YOU BIDDING ON THE WRONG KEYWORDS?

I've had clients attempt to bid on specific keyword types, such as the name of an online tool, because they hoped the platform's customers might be interested in their service.

Sadly, *hope* will get you nowhere with Google.

The lack of clicks will lead to Google 'rewarding' you with a low Quality Score.

KEYWORDS WITH A DOUBLE MEANING

Could your keywords be used for other purposes? I've had a client seeking to bid on keywords such as "sales trainers", only for Google to match it against people who want to buy shoes!

Sometimes, no matter how hard an agency or consultant might try, the Quality Score will never rise above 5. The keywords are used by different people in different circumstances. So while we might want a high Quality Score, that's not always achievable.

3. IMPRESSION SHARE AND CLICK SHARE

Add your impression and click share at your campaign level as additional columns by ticking all the boxes shown in the following screenshot.

Impression share shows how often your ads appear in the top four results and in the top position. Keep an eye on it to check if your ads are displayed too low to get many clicks.

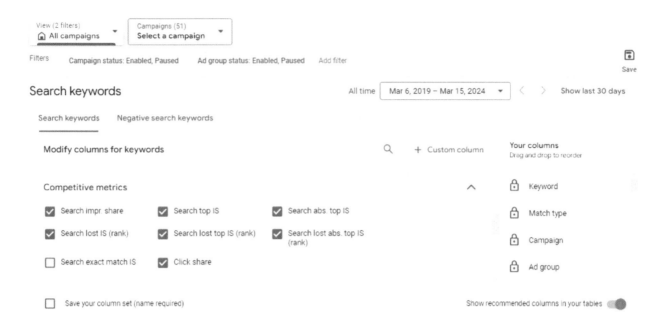

Lost impression share shows how your low Quality Score and budget affect your visibility. If your Quality Score is costing you impressions, you'll see it in this column.

The click share shows how many of the available clicks you acquired. It only includes impressions where you've entered the ad auction. It wouldn't be included if your ad didn't appear due to a low Quality Score or budget.

4. ADD MORE NEGATIVE KEYWORDS - NO, EVEN MORE!

In my early years of running Google Ads, I was employed as a consultant to a florist. My sole task? Do nothing but add *hundreds* of negative keywords. These days, adding negative keywords is an essential part of our process.

In fact, over time, your negative keyword list will grow to have 500-1000 keywords. Yes, you read that right!

Adding negative keywords will increase your click-through rate and improve your Quality Score.

I've seen cases in which adding hundreds of negative keywords caused a massive CTR jump overnight.

Don't underestimate how important negative keywords are to your campaign. More importantly, remember that it's an *ongoing process* – you need to add more negative keywords regularly.

If you've been running Google Ads in the past, go through all your search terms and compile the biggest list you possibly can.

5. CHANGE MAX CONVERSIONS TO TARGET CPA

After you've run your account for a while and established a cost per conversion, you can ask Google to start bringing the cost down with Target CPA (cost per acquisition) bidding.

To do this, go into the Campaigns under the Campaigns tab, select the campaign you want to edit, and click "Edit" to "Change bid strategy". Select Maximise Conversions as your bid strategy and adjust it to Target CPA.

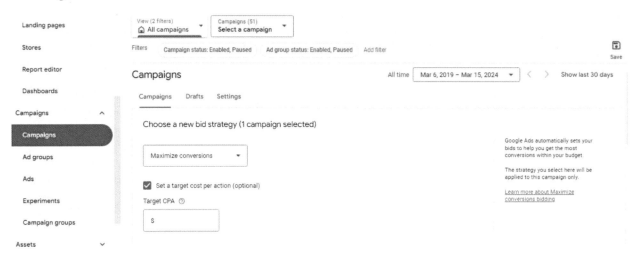

Google may suggest a potential target CPA for you. If it's higher than you'd like to pay, consider ignoring it and bidding a little less than its suggestion.

If Google doesn't suggest a potential CPA for you, add your desired CPA.

It's important to understand that moving to target CPA from Maximise Conversions can drop the number of impressions you are receiving. I've often seen ads stop showing completely. If this happens to you, leave it for 24 hours and then see if the problem corrects itself. If it does not, you will need to increase the target CPA to allow Google the bandwidth to show your ads.

Since target CPA is managed by Google's AI, it will take some time to optimise. Avoid changing it too often. I typically advise my clients not to change it more than once per week to give Google AI a chance to work its magic.

Be aware that if you only want to bid for mobile or desktop, target CPA will remove device targeting. That's why it's sometimes tricky for B2B advertisers to implement effectively.

MONITOR YOUR COMPETITORS

Competitor behaviour will affect your campaigns. Keep an eye on them.

However, don't try to constantly take the top spot in Google results. It's a fool's game. Focus on the cost per lead or sale instead.

AUCTION INSIGHTS

Auction Insights show you which keywords you and competitors have in common.

AD COPY

Keep an eye on your competitors' ad copy! Check if they're making new claims or introducing new discounts.

CLICK FRAUD

Unfortunately, there's fraud in everything. In the PPC world, we call the practice of clicking others' ads to use their budget and remove them from the ad auction "click fraud".

You can check if you've been a victim of click fraud by adding the "Invalid Clicks" column at the campaign level. Fortunately, Google can tell when somebody clicks on your ad repeatedly, so it will refund your cost per click.

If you have over 20% invalid clicks, you could be a victim of click fraud. Although Google refunds you for these clicks, in my experience it doesn't detect the same amount of clicks again.

Sometimes invalid clicks make sense. A prospect could click your ad multiple times, especially if you have sitelinks. It is also likely to happen with remarketing campaigns, where people see your ads multiple times.

Unfortunately, there's not a lot you can do about it. There are click fraud tools, but they typically alert you of clicks that Google's already detected. If you get lots of invalid clicks, it's worth raising your concerns with Google.

At the end of the day, the benefits of Google Ads outweigh the cons. Even with click fraud, your clicks are refunded. Plus, there are often creative ways to circumvent aggressive competitors.

Ultimately, achieving Google Ads success is an ongoing process. There *are* things you can set and forget. But you need to manage your Google Ads account to make the most of it.

As we learn more about our prospects, we need to refine our ads.

One client I've worked with started by using one landing page per ad group.

As her business grew, we realised we could get even better results by building location-specific landing pages.

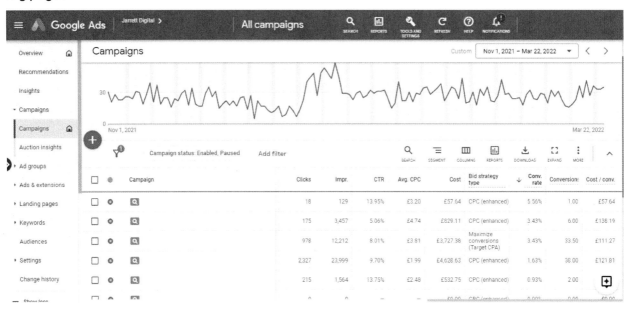

As a specialist in a particular type of therapy, she considered testing general, location-based keywords. Thankfully, she got in touch with me, and we avoided that. It would've been the worst thing for her ad performance.

Instead, we picked her specific therapy type, which her leads were highly motivated to join.

Once we launched her specific landing pages, we started generating leads effectively. Even though the conversion and cost figures listed don't reflect all the leads that came through WhatsApp or social media thanks to her Google Ads, she was *thrilled*.

We were proud, too. After all, it's hard *not* to be proud when you deliver **10x ROI – £10,000 for every £1,000 spent**.

One of the techniques you might want to consider next is remarketing, a personal favourite of mine. Interested? Read on!

CHAPTER 7
REMARKETING

Now that you're getting sales, it's time to capture visitors who may have seen your landing page at the wrong time.

Is it finally the right time? Remarketing helps us find out!

I've loved Remarketing Ads ever since their infancy. I recall coming across my then three-year-old excitedly clicking on pictures of "mummy" on a computer. I still remember her excitement at seeing them everywhere.

Even today, I love hearing clients tell me they just got off the phone with a new customer who said:

> *"I've been seeing your ads everywhere and **knew** I just had to pick up the phone and call!"*

Remarketing increases familiarity with your brand, makes it more likely that a prospect will convert, encourages current customers to refer your business, and stimulates repeat purchases.

What's *not* to love?

And if you consider that 97% of visitors never return to a website without remarketing[5], then it becomes a fantastic way to capture the conversions you thought you'd lost.

Sadly, remarketing may not be around for much longer due to Google's recent privacy updates. I may even have to remove it from the future editions of this book. So use it while you still can!

---

[5] https://mailchimp.com/resources/what-is-retargeting/

WHAT EXACTLY IS REMARKETING?

Remarketing is the practice of following visitors across the web with your ads after they have visited your website and received a pixel.

Please note that we'll also look at 'following' your email subscribers and YouTube viewers through remarketing in this chapter. It's going to significantly increase brand recognition and boost your conversions!

SOME BUSINESSES CAN'T USE REMARKETING

However, only certain types of businesses benefit from remarketing. So, before you read any further, let's make sure your business isn't a bad fit.

Businesses where decisions are made in the same visit (e.g., emergency services such as locksmiths, electricians or plumbers) aren't a good fit for remarketing.

Similarly, certain industries can't use remarketing because Google protects the searchers' privacy (for example, health services like hypnotherapy or drug rehab services)[6].

Generally, any industry or ad where you'd use someone's sensitive interests or personal hardships – for example, divorce coaching, alcohol, gambling, or negative financial status is out of the question.

If you don't tick any of these boxes, keep reading!

HOW TO SET UP YOUR REMARKETING AUDIENCES

There are two ways to create remarketing audiences:

1. Use a Google remarketing pixel and add it to your website or Google Tag Manager.
2. Link your Google Analytics account to Google Ads and use Google Analytics visitors as a remarketing audience.

I like to link both, as I sometimes notice slight differences in the numbers of available audience members when using each method.

---

[6] https://support.google.com/adspolicy/answer/143465?hl=en&ref_topic=1626336

If you want to set up the Google remarketing pixel, you'll find it under "Tools" and "Audience manager". Go to "Your Data Sources", select the "Google Ads Tag" and follow the instructions to install the pixel (or hire a professional).

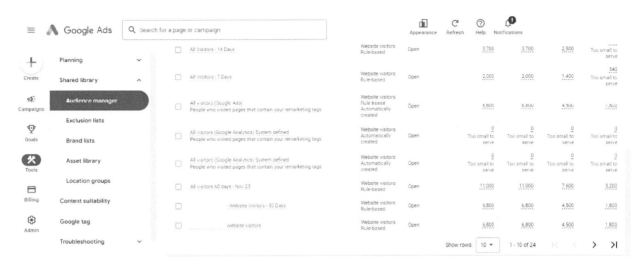

Once you've installed the pixel, your audience will start to fill up with visitors. You'll need to acquire a certain number of audience members before you can remarket to them.

To add in the Google Analytics audience, select "Google Analytics (UA)" in "Your Data Sources" and follow the instructions to link them. Again, it'll take a while to acquire the minimum audience size.

The audiences created at this stage include everyone that visits your website, so bear this in mind. This is good because both your organic traffic and traffic coming from other sources will be followed by your ads.

However, remember that – at this stage – we don't know what they're interested in or which of your pages they visited. So if you want to advertise to this large audience size, you'll need to build generic Remarketing Ads.

If you want more specific ads, set up specific audiences and build display ads relevant to the pages they visited. You can build them by clicking the "Segments" tab and adding individual pages (or series of pages) to the website visitors' section.

REMARKETING TO ALL CONVERTERS

Google automatically creates an audience of everyone who has converted. It gets this data from what it knows about the conversions you set up, so it's crucial to set them up correctly.

This is a good audience because you'll be able to remarket various ads to people interested in your service.

ADDING YOUR YOUTUBE VIEWERS AND SUBSCRIBERS

You can also add your YouTube users as an audience. However, you need to create the link between your YouTube account and your Google Ads account to access this. If you haven't done it yet, go to "Your Data Sources".

If you have a lot of YouTube activity, you can select only the people who liked your video or who subscribed to your channel.

Please keep in mind that you don't have to retarget YouTube viewers with a YouTube ad. You'll be able to follow them with your image ads just the same as you follow your website visitors.

UPLOADING EMAIL LISTS

If you have an opted-in email list, you'll love this section!

Email lists work perfectly for many of my clients. For example, clients who offer business insurance or business broadband services remarket around their clients' renewal dates. SaaS clients offer free trials to encourage their prospects to convert into paying customers, or they encourage their existing clients to upgrade.

There are so many potential uses for remarketing to your mailing list subscribers, and I see hardly anybody talking about this topic!

At the very least, consider uploading your email list of past clients or past subscribers and update it regularly. (Most tools will automate this for you.)

Go to the Audience manager again. Then, click the plus button to add new, and select "Customer list". You can upload a file with all the addresses. Google will then match your email list against its records (linking to Google accounts) and tell you what percentage of these people you can target with remarketing. This process can take up to 24 hours.

Don't expect a 100% match rate. Your remarketing segment will never be as large as your original email list. Instead, it'll vary between 50% and 100%.

When revising your segments after a while, you may notice that Google creates similar audiences. These work similarly to Facebook Lookalike Audiences. Personally, I haven't had a huge amount of success advertising with similar audiences created by Google, but that may change with Google's new campaign types.

Never say never!

HOW TO CREATE REMARKETING ADS

Now that we've set up your audiences, it's time to create your Remarketing Ads!

Create a new campaign as you normally would. The first option you'll come across is "Audience segments". Select your retargeting segment or create one now in Audience manager using the previous instructions.

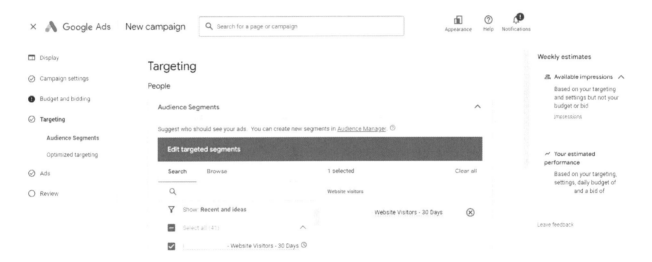

Once you set up your ad, decide on your **frequency capping** – i.e., how often can a single audience member see your ad during their membership duration? If your customers purchase your products regularly (for example, a skincare shop), you can show your ads more often.

Go to Campaigns, then the Settings, and select the campaign you want to add frequency capping to. It will be in "Additional settings".

In terms of ad creatives, Remarketing Ads are similar to Responsive Search Ads. You have to add various headlines and descriptions.

You'll also be asked to upload images, including logos. Scan Twitter, Facebook and your website to find images if you don't have any suitable ones. In my opinion, it's always worth ordering a set of branded visuals from a designer.

Most advertisers at this stage will set up a basic ad that redirects to a single landing page or a homepage. Make sure your new images match the brand that your visitors initially saw, so they recognise it.

I've had clients succeed with discount codes that take people through to a dedicated landing page. It's great because you'll be able to track where they originally came from. Using discount codes is up to you. Only you know if offering a discount code suits your brand or service at this stage.

To create your campaign, click "Create a campaign without guidance" and select one of your remarketing audiences as your audience.

From there, the set-up is similar to any Google ad.

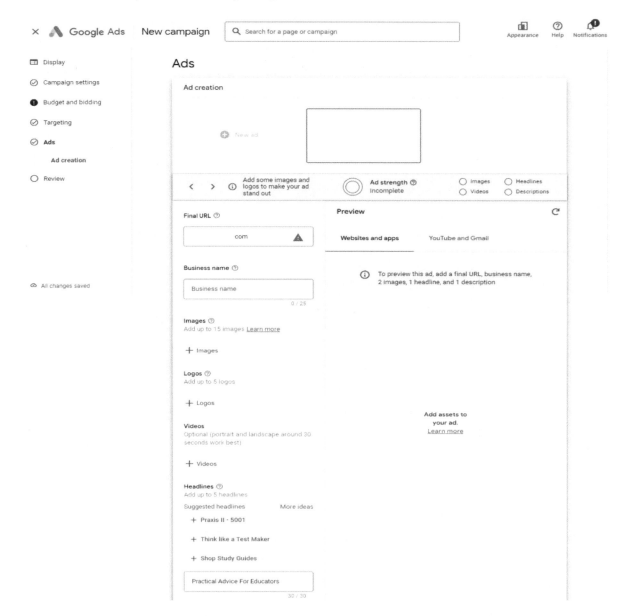

Use the title case and add one or two testimonials in the description section.

Pay attention to the original offer that made the person visit your landing page. Identify the most appealing elements and then double down on them in your Remarketing Ad.

Remarketing Ads in the right hands can be extremely powerful for your business, especially if you rely on first-party data such as mailing lists.

You can stay top of mind and, with further customisation, even create customised ad combinations based on various parameters and preferences.

After all, you run a fantastic business. Google Ads simply helps you prove it to even more customers!

CHAPTER 8
SHOPPING ADS

If you're advertising physical products, whether to sell them locally or through eCommerce, you'll want to explore Google's Shopping Ads. Make sure you've set up your Google Merchant Centre account first! Getting down to business, my recommendation is to **reiterate** by **selecting the standard Shopping campaign.**

Now, you might be wondering: *"Wait, Claire, aren't you going to encourage us to use Performance Max?"*

I'll be honest — **I don't recommend using Performance Max at this stage.** It offers very little control, your ads pop up on different channels without rhyme or reason, and it takes over all your brand traffic — only to declare that it's bringing in a lot of sales! It's a very poor form of account management, so skip it. Instead, **create multiple campaigns — one for each product type that you offer.**

HOW TO SET UP YOUR GOOGLE SHOPPING AD CAMPAIGN

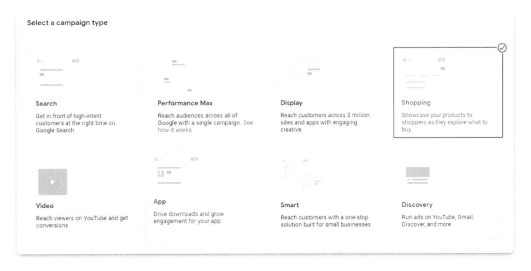

Now here comes the fun part!

You'll **create 1 ad group per product or product group.** Select them from the drop-down menu based on your Google Merchant Centre integration. Google Ads will tackle this automatically for you by looking through your catalogue and sorting by ID, brand, type, etc.

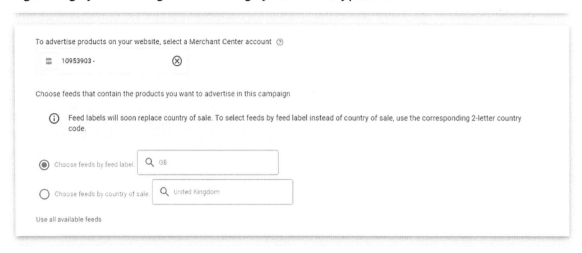

For example, if you sell trainers for women and trainers for men, you could set up 2 distinct ad groups. Alternatively, if you sell both Nike and Adidas trainers, you could set up 1 ad group for *each*.

The goal is to distinguish between different product types, so you can easily monitor performance and identify your top-performing products.

BIDDING, LOCATIONS, NETWORKS AND DEVICES

The good news is that cost per click is much lower for Google Shopping Ads!

Select your bids manually and add your target CPC. Since the costs are much lower, start slow. Bid just a few pence (or cents – depending on where you're based).

We'll exclude the "Search network" as we do with a standard campaign – we want to make sure our clicks are targeted, not scattered.

Make sure you pinpoint the best-performing locations as well!

IMPORTANT NOTE ON THE PRODUCT SELECTION

Now here comes the crucial part – the single place I see most advertisers (and agencies) fail with Shopping Ads:

Don't let Google add automation to your product selection.

When reviewing the products Google has selected for you, modify the "Everything Else" option to exclude all the products that you do **not** want in your campaign.

HOW TO OPTIMISE YOUR SHOPPING AD CAMPAIGNS

Set your campaigns live – but don't think you're done! Just because you have launched your Shopping Ads, it doesn't mean you can be laissez-faire about it.

Monitor your campaigns daily.

If negative keywords are crucial for all Google Ads campaigns, then they're even more essential for Shopping Ads. Since there are no keywords per se for Shopping Ads, Google will be guessing which keywords apply to your product based on your descriptions.

Guessing costs money – and I don't want you wasting your budget!

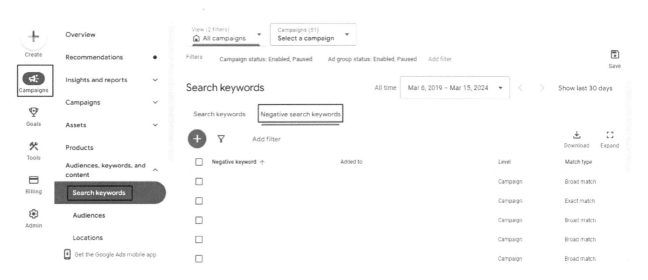

So keep Google under control by ensuring that it's only displaying your products for relevant queries by **adding negative keywords daily.**

You'll find them in the "Audiences, keywords and content" -> "Negative search terms" section. Select the keywords you'd like to exclude and add them to your negative keywords list.

OPTIMISING YOUR SHOPPING ADS BUDGET

In some cases, your ads might not show or you might realise that you're not spending your entire daily budget.

The fix is really simple: increase your bids slightly until your ads start to show.

And once the data pours in, it'll be time to **switch to one of my favourite types of bidding – target ROAS (return on ad spend).**

You'll enter a figure you want as your return on advertising spend. For example, if you enter a target ROAS of 800%, Google will aim to deliver $8 for every $1 you spend.

The ideal ROAS is very personal to your company. I've had clients who were over the moon with a 300% ROAS, while others were only satisfied with 2500%.

Of course – aim for the moon. Even if you fall, you'll land among the stars!

CATALOGUE OPTIMISATION

Other than adjusting your bidding and ensuring that your negative keywords list is as precise as possible, your next area of optimisation will be **your product catalogue:**

- Which products have the highest margin?
- Which products are your best-sellers for Shopping Ads?

And so on! As you learn which products are your top performers, I recommend **increasing the bids for the ones with a higher margin.**

Similarly, consider reducing the bids for those with lower margins. You can set all of this up in the "Product groups" section by editing each group and clicking the '+' sign that appears on the right side of the box.

Ultimately, **you'll get much better returns by cherry-picking the products that drive the most revenue to your business** instead of letting Google take the reins. I can assure you, it won't discriminate between products. Instead, it'll advertise your entire feed – even the products that may not work well in terms of PPC.

After all, it has no concerns about your budget.

ARE YOU READY TO WIN AT GOOGLE ADS?

When I first started my journey with Google Ads 17 years ago, it wasn't a very well-known platform. Not like it is today. With my background in teaching, I saw a huge opportunity to master it and then share what I learned with others.

Now 17 years later, I can easily say that I am still as passionate about teaching others as when I first started. This is because I get to have a huge impact on my clients' and students' businesses, which is incredibly rewarding.

I particularly like working with smaller businesses because that's where I can have an even bigger impact on people's lives. When working with companies with hundreds of staff, there isn't anybody in particular who feels the impact of the campaigns and tells you about it. Sure – the C suite is pleased about the numbers and they go on to sign up with me on large retainers, which is great.

But it's not the same as changing the lives of people at smaller businesses. Having them call me and say, "Claire – you have changed my life. I just put my son into private school because of the extra money we're making. He was really struggling at school, and now he is happier than ever." I just never get tired of hearing stuff like that. It's why I do what I do.

Now that you have finished the book and can see the potential impact of its blueprint, I want to extend an invitation for us to continue our work together.

When I first got started with Google Ads, the search was clunky. We spent *days* researching keywords that meant the difference between breaking even and making a profit. Today, the advertising world has changed and it continues to evolve. You have already got a leg up over your competition because you read this book.

But some of my students choose to delve deeper into their ads with me – having me go through their campaigns with them and helping to make necessary corrections.

One of these students is Mary, the relationship coach who signed up for personal Google Ads coaching with me. She saw 10x ROI.

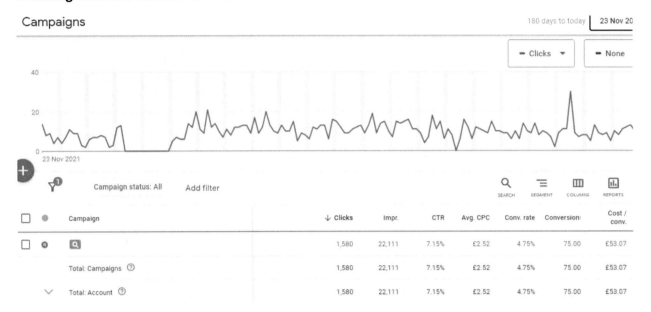

Mary went through all the steps I've outlined in this book. From creating landing pages specific to keywords, to building different ad groups.

Then, she booked private coaching with me and we optimised together. We added negative keywords to avoid people who weren't her ideal customers. We refined her offer to include such *detail* that conversions started pouring in.

And then, we made sure that for every £400 she was spending, she was bringing in a £4000 return.

As I've mentioned before, I've been working with Google Ads for the past 17 years. Some of the coaches active today were originally trained by me (as were many Google Ads agencies owners), and I was the first person in Europe to offer Google AdWords training courses.

But my work goes beyond your Google Ads account.

Google Ads leads are not created equally. The biggest impact my work consistently creates is impossible to measure by looking at the data inside of your Google Ads account. It is subjective and can only be measured in terms of lead quality.

Google Ads cannot easily measure lead quality. The numbers inside your account will never give you the answers to the two questions that are truly important for your business:

1. How do I repel customers that are wasting my/my team's time, and who don't spend very much?
2. How do I consistently attract high-quality customers that go on to spend large sums of money with my business?

I am demonstrating the answers to both of these questions with the words you are currently reading.

You do not improve lead quality by solely focusing on the numbers inside your account. You improve lead quality through better messaging and the top-level strategy that sits behind your keywords and campaigns.

Lead quality can only be measured by:

- The impact on your business bank account after your campaigns have been launched,
- The quality of the people that you go on to work with, and
- The lifetime value of your customers.

This is what makes my approach unique. I combine the objective (data inside your Google Ads account) with the subjective (the way you communicate with your leads).

This is the stuff that is challenging to learn, let alone teach. But it's incredibly important, and it's this kind of marketing psychology that will dramatically move the needle – shaping your business's growth.

The major problem with how most people approach Google Ads is that the actual campaign builds are handed off to lower members of their teams who don't understand the bigger picture.

They are too focused on the data, rather than attracting the right kind of client that will help their businesses hit their goals.

Another thing I find when talking to people is that people are too focused on their ads, and not enough on their websites. This is a critical flaw in thinking.

Your website has a massive impact on the success of your Google Ads account.

By aligning your website's messaging with the keywords inside your account, it will increase the quality score inside of your Google Ads account – this can make the difference between paying $1 and $10 for a single click.

My work is always tailored to each client's specific needs. I believe that any good Google Ads management professional will tailor their plan to fit the needs of each client. This approach is especially important in marketing, where every customer thinks differently to the next. If you'd like my team to manage your ads for you (as you'll be so busy from incoming work), then this is also something we can discuss.

Our approach to Google Ads management is just like teaching through asking questions – it's the only way to really get to the bottom of things. That way, my students arrive at the answers themselves – ensuring that they internalise what is being taught.

I hope you have enjoyed this book, and if you're interested in learning more about my managed Done For You services, then you can book a 30-minute discovery call at www.clairejarrett.com/contact.

If you already have a Google Ads account and want my team to perform a complimentary audit (before or after you've made the changes recommended in this book), then you can book at www. clairejarrett.com/get-audit.

> You can also sign up for **FREE lifetime updates** of this book
> at www.clairejarrett.com/google-ads-book.

Made in the USA
Las Vegas, NV
13 December 2024

14184332R00057